We are endowed with the wealth of our land and its natural wonders. We enjoy a resourceful and enterprising spirit and have an ever increasing awareness of our prosperity and good fortune to be Americans. Every one of us has the opportunity and responsibility to build, preserve and defend our nation's freedoms for ourselves and future generations. As we stand to salute our flag

OLD GLORY

appreciate all that we have and all that this flag stands for. Take great pride in being an American.

Old Glory remains our unifying symbol:

It is a constant reminder that we, as Americans, are a most fortunate people.

My heart is turning home

The red, white and blue of our "Stars and Stripes"
is proudly displayed by freedom-loving
Americans on our national capitol, state houses,
schools and homes.

and there I long to be

Across our land, throughout the world, and thousands of miles into space, our glorious American Flag symbolizes our dedication to being the leader of the free world.

Our brave soldiers were tested during several more monumental occasions during the twentieth century, proudly carrying our American banner to foreign shores. Our courageous young men and women fought and served so that others might enjoy democracy and freedom.

Flanked by two World Wars, the Great Depression allowed the American people to prove their resilience through resourcefulness and a strong work ethic.

The American Spirit preserved our nation during the first half of the twentieth century as many Americans struggled to overcome our internal economic conflicts.

The United States encountered many
trials as it grew.
Our sons were called to fight
in distant lands to keep the
world safe for democracy and
for all people.
During the first and second
World Wars, our brave soldiers
fought for freedom from
the tyrants and dictators of
foreign lands.

Sweet land of Liberty

The United States became a strong
and diverse land, welcoming people
from different countries
with diverse ethnic backgrounds
who were searching for more freedom,
more liberty, and a better way of life.

They were proud to
become Americans!

Tragically, during Lincoln's administration, brother fought against brother with unsurpassed courage for what each believed in. After four years the North and the South resolved the conflict and our nation was once again united.

Abraham Lincoln, our sixteenth president, is remembered as one of our greatest statesmen. It was he who inherited the unenviable task of preserving our nation.

In one of his most famous speeches he eloquently stated that "our fathers brought forth upon this continent a new nation conceived in liberty, and dedicated to the proposition that all men are created equal".

...and our country expanded its boundaries from "sea to shining sea".

During the nineteenth century, brave independent pioneers blazed our frontiers . . .

These gallant men were dedicated to the idealism of creating a nation where everyone, regardless of race, color, or creed, is equal and has unalienable rights to life, liberty, and the pursuit of happiness.

These ideals important

remain just as today.

George Washington
is known as the
"Father of Our Country".
His strength, courage
and fortitude
became examples for
the men he led.

... men fought for liberty and freedom against odds that seemed almost insurmountable.

From the very beginning of our conflict with England . . .

Over two hundred years ago our forefathers took a stand for what they believed in.

They declared their independence from a mighty power, a country much stronger than our original thirteen colonies.

When you see our glorious flag, the symbol of our country, enjoy the moment. Take time to reflect on how proud you are to be an American.

America, America
God shed
his grace on thee
And crown thy good
with brotherhood
from sea to shining sea.

KATHARINE LEE BATES

Presented to:

_____

On this day:

_____

From:

_____

A Tribute
To Our Nation's Flag

Through the years many beautiful songs have been written to acknowledge the special place that Americans hold in their hearts for their symbol of freedom— "Old Glory". This book is a new song— a symphony of words and American folk art blended together. May it strike a chord of patriotism within you... beating true "for the red, white, and blue".

This book is dedicated to those who share in the goal of rekindling and preserving the spirit, pride and respect for our nation. Its traditions, heritage and freedoms are symbolized by our grand flag...

OLD GLORY

With deep appreciation I would like to thank my wife, Susanne, my family and all of my friends at Lang for understanding and supporting my vision.
I would also like to share my sincere appreciation with Susan Winget for these glorious illustrations and to Roxie Kelley and Mark Kimball Moulton for their final thoughts on these words about OLD GLORY.

Text by Robert Lang
Paintings by Susan Winget
Copyright 1999
All Rights Reserved

Published by Lang Books
A division of
R.A. Lang Card Co. Ltd.
514 Wells Street
Delafield, WI 53018
262-646-2211
www.lang.com

10 9 8 7 6 5 4 3 2
ISBN: 0-7412-0435-5

Old Glory...

an American Treasure

Written by Robert Lang

Paintings by Susan Winget

Lang Books ... a Lang Company

Delafield, W.I.

To Mrs Kessler,
We hope you and all the children in your
classroom enjoy this wonderful Book.
love, Ford Lockyer